DRAWING
Ocean Animals

BY ABBY COLICH
ILLUSTRATED BY JUAN CALLE

CAPSTONE PRESS
a capstone imprint

Snap books are published by Capstone Press, an imprint of Capstone
1710 Roe Crest Drive, North Mankato, Minnesota 56003
www.capstonepub.com

Copyright © 2015 by Capstone Press, a Capstone imprint. All rights reserved. No part of this publication may be reproduced in whole or in part, or stored in a retrieval system, or transmitted in any form or by any means, electronic, mechanical, photocopying, recording, or otherwise, without written permission of the publisher.

Library of Congress Cataloging-in-Publication Data
Colich, Abby, author.
 Drawing ocean animals / Written by Abby Colich ; Illustrated by Juan Calle.
   pages cm. — (Drawing amazing animals)
 ISBN 978-1-4914-2131-4 (library binding)
Summary: "Gives readers easy instructions on how to draw different animals of the ocean"— Provided by publisher.
1. Marine animals in art—Juvenile literature. 2. Drawing—Technique—Juvenile literature. I. Calle, Juan, 1977- illustrator. II. Title.
 NC781.C65 2015
 743.6—dc23
                              2014033156

Editorial Credits
Juliette Peters and Charmaine Whitman, designers
Aruna Rangarajan, cover designer
Laura Manthe, production specialist

Photo Credits
Design elements by Shutterstock

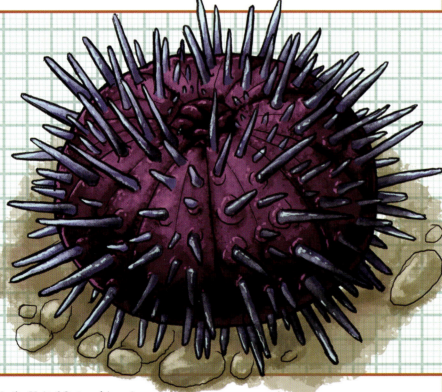

Printed in the United States of America
in North Mankato, Minnesota.
092014   008482CGS15

Table of Contents

Getting Started 4
Tools of the Trade 5
Sea Star 6
Sea Anemone 8
Clown Fish 10
Orca 12
Octopus 14
Narwhal 16
Jellyfish 18
Sea Horse 20
Sea Urchin 22
Bottlenose Dolphin Family 24
Coral Reef 28

Internet Sites 32

Getting Started

From a playful family of dolphins to colorful coral reefs, the ocean is full of amazing animals. Animals are fun to learn about and fun to draw too. Whether you're skilled at sketching or new to the world of drawing, you can have fun filling pages with a wide variety of sea creatures.

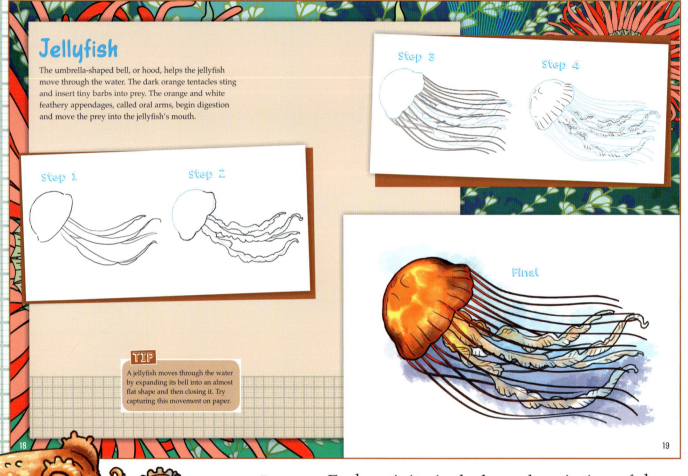

Each activity includes a description of the animal, steps to show you exactly how to draw each creature, and a tip for when you want to get creative and mix things up. If your clown fish is a joke or your narwhal is a no-go, don't worry. Drawing takes practice. If you mess up, it's OK to start over again. Just remember to be creative and have fun while you work.

Tools of the Trade

Drawing is a fun and inexpensive way to express yourself and your creativity. Before you get started, be sure you have the proper tools.

Paper
Any white paper will work, but a sketchbook meant just for drawing is best.

Pencils
Any pencil will do, but many artists prefer graphite pencils made especially for drawing.

Color
A good set of colored pencils will give you many options for color. You can also try using markers or paint. Many artists enjoy outlining and filling in their work with artist pens.

Sharpener
Your pencils will be getting a lot of use, so be sure you have a sturdy sharpener. A good sharpener will give your pencil a nice, sharp point.

Eraser
Be sure to get a good eraser. Choose an eraser that won't leave smudges on your clean, white paper.

Electronics
Many great apps and programs allow you to draw on screen rather than on paper. If you want to give this medium a try, have an adult help you get started. Learn all the features and functions before you begin.

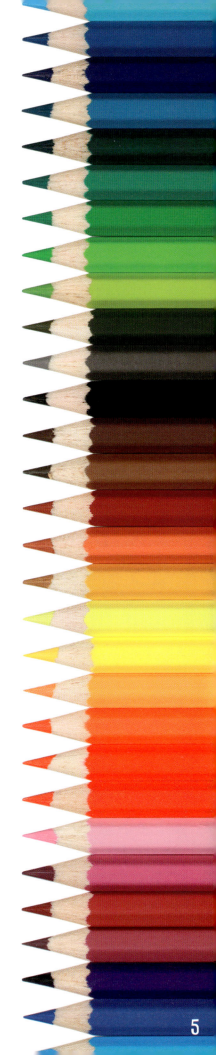

Sea Star

This faceless, brainless creature may seem simple, but the sea star is anything but. This animal has two stomachs—one that digests food and one that releases from its mouth to capture prey. Hundreds of tiny tube feet along a sea star's arms help it move through the water.

Step 1

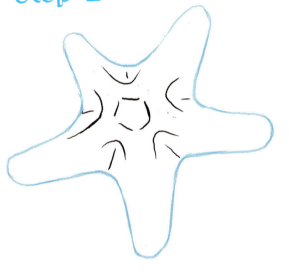

Step 2

TIP

Have you ever seen a sea star with its arms bent, clinging to a rock? Tube feet help with this too. Try capturing this action on paper.

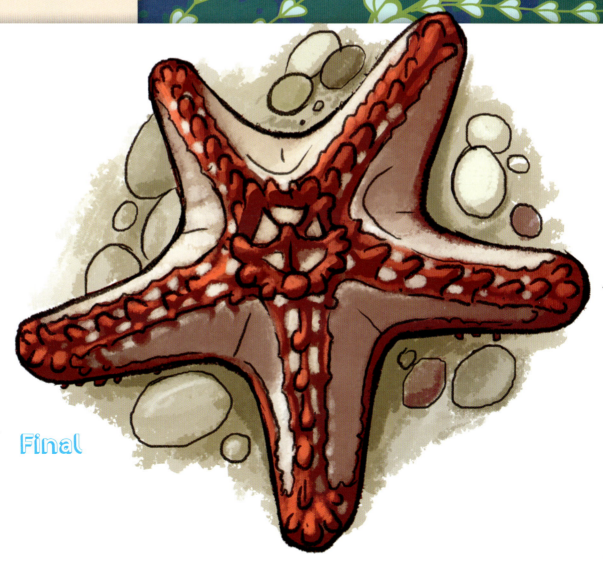

Sea Anemone

Sea anemones spend most of their time attached to rocks or coral reefs. The growths coming out of their bodies are stinging tentacles. An anemone will wait for prey to come by, sting the prey with its tentacles, and then guide the meal into its mouth.

Step 1

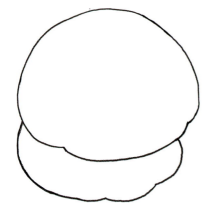

Step 2

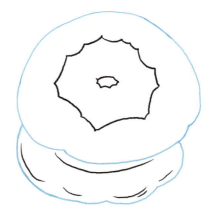

TIP

Give your sea anemone some height by drawing it a taller body. Some anemones can be up to 6 feet (1.8 meters) tall.

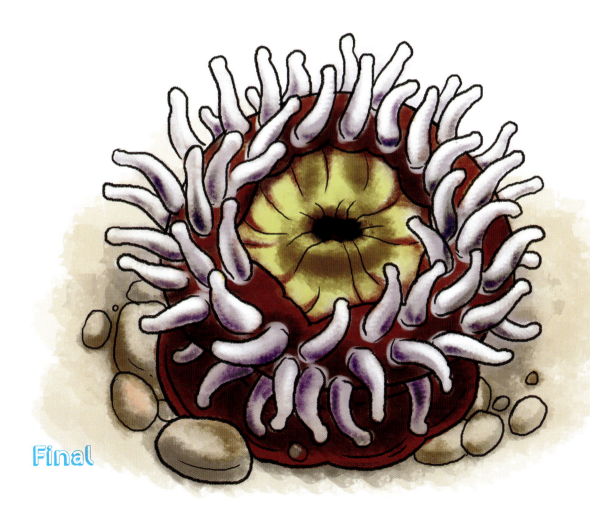
Final

Clown Fish

Beautiful, bright-orange clown fish are adorned with white stripes along their heads, bodies, and tails. Each stripe is outlined in black. A clown fish's bright skin warns predators to stay away.

Step 1

Step 2

TIP

Clown fish live among sea anemones. A coat of mucus protects the fish's bodies from the anemones' stings. Try drawing these two sea creatures together.

Step 3

Step 4

Final

Orca

Orcas, commonly called killer whales, are actually a species of dolphin. The largest of all dolphins, these huge creatures can grow to nearly the size of a school bus. All orcas have black bodies with white markings. Each orca can be identified by its own pattern.

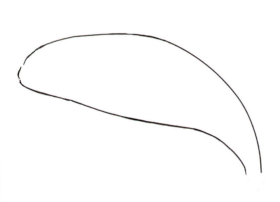
Step 1

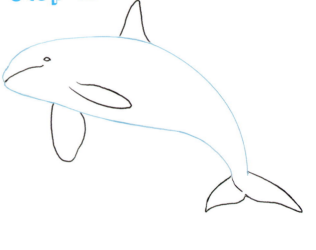
Step 2

TIP

Orcas travel in groups called pods. After you learn to draw one orca, try drawing several of them together.

Final

Octopus

Scientists consider the octopus to be the smartest of all invertebrates. Among its many defenses from predators, an octopus can change colors to blend in with its surroundings. It also squeezes into tiny spaces and squirts clouds of ink to hide behind.

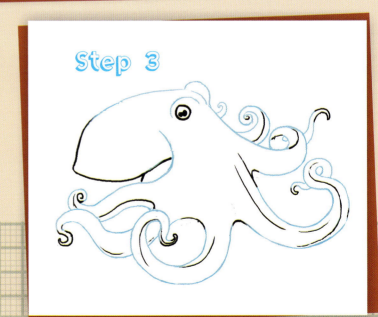

TIP
Once you master the octopus, draw it performing one of its amazing defenses.

Step 4

Step 5

Final

Narwhal

People rarely see narwhals in the wild, but that doesn't mean you can't become a master narwhal artist. You can see why this creature is called "the unicorn of the sea." Its long horn is actually a tooth. The tooth grows into a tusk straight through a male narwhal's upper lip.

Step 1

Step 2

TIP

Be sure to draw your narwhal in an icy habitat. Narwhals only live in or near the Arctic Ocean.

Step 3

Step 4

Final

Jellyfish

The umbrella-shaped bell, or hood, helps the jellyfish move through the water. The dark orange tentacles sting and insert tiny barbs into prey. The orange and white feathery appendages, called oral arms, begin digestion and move the prey into the jellyfish's mouth.

Step 1

Step 2

TIP

A jellyfish moves through the water by expanding its bell into an almost flat shape and then closing it. Try capturing this movement on paper.

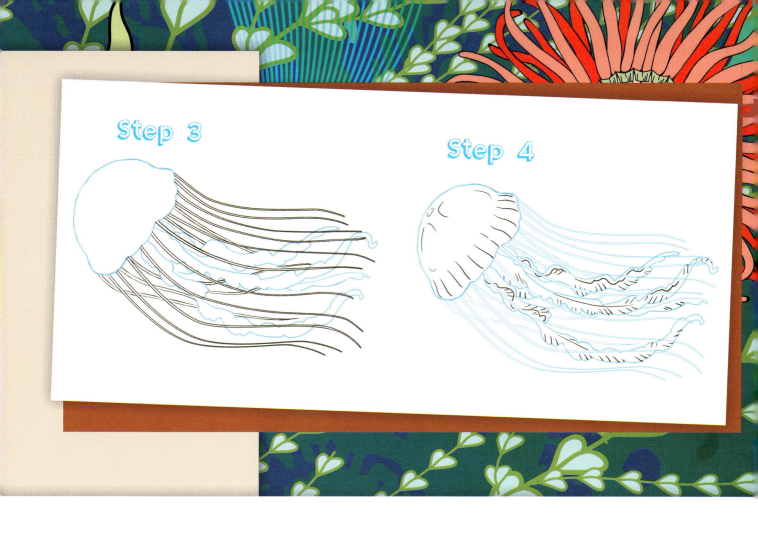
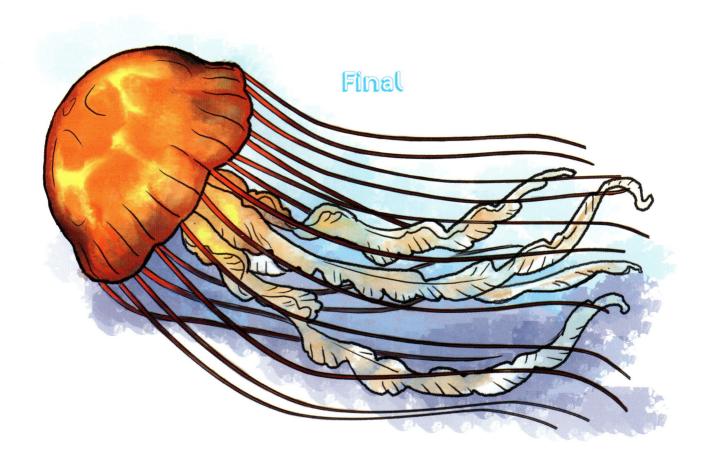

19

Sea Horse

You can easily see how the sea horse got its name. This animal uses the little fin on its back to swim, but it doesn't go very fast. So it spends most of its time using its monkey-shaped tail to hang on to sea grass and coral.

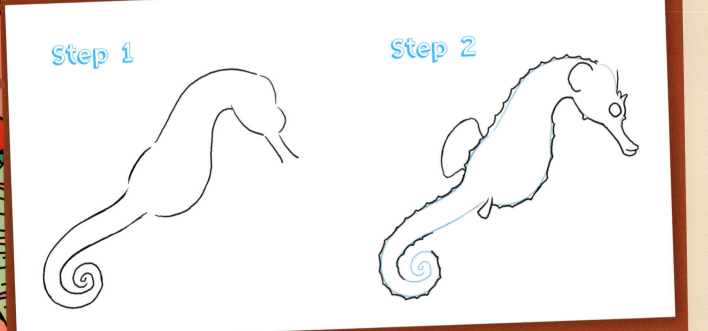

TIP

A sea horse must eat almost constantly to stay alive. Try drawing your sea horse munching on a shrimp.

Sea Urchin

Sea urchins look a bit like pincushions. The spines sticking out of their bodies help them move along the seafloor. The spines are also filled with venom, which helps protect the creatures from predators. Despite this defense, they can still become food for fish and sea otters.

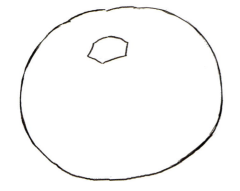
Step 1

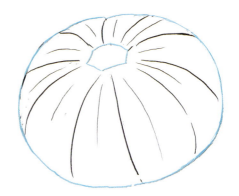
Step 2

TIP

Sea urchins are actually a relative of sea stars. Draw some of these creatures hanging out together on the ocean floor.

Step 3

Step 4

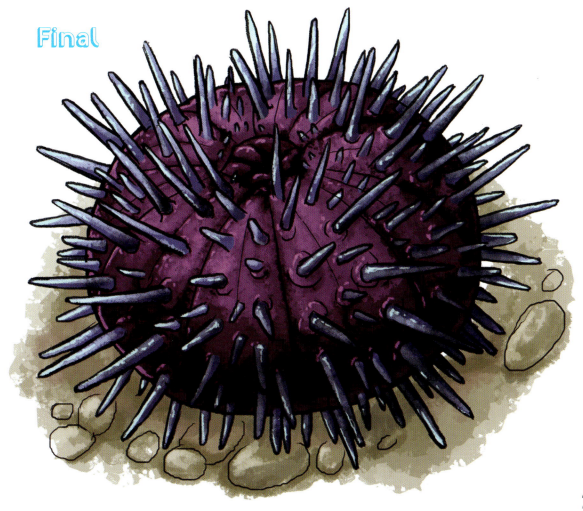

Final

23

Bottlenose Dolphin Family

Why do so many people love dolphins? One reason is that their curved mouths make them look like they are always smiling. You usually won't spot a dolphin alone. They live in groups of 10 to 30 called pods.

Step 1

Step 2

Step 3

Step 4

TIP

Dolphins must come up to the surface of the water often to breathe. Try drawing a dolphin jumping out of the water.

continued on next page

Final

Coral Reef

Millions of tiny animals called polyps form vast coral reefs in tropical waters. As polyps grow, they leave behind a hard skeleton. Together the skeletons create large, rocklike structures. Coral reefs are home to a wide array of creatures that form a diverse ecosystem.

Step 1

Step 2

Step 3

Step 4

TIP

Many creatures live on or near coral reefs, including shrimp, sea turtles, and jellyfish. Try adding one or two of these to your illustration.

continued on next page

Internet Sites

FactHound offers a safe, fun way to find Internet sites related to this book. All of the sites on FactHound have been researched by our staff.

Here's all you do:

Visit www.facthound.com

Type in this code: 9781491421314

Check out projects, games and lots more at www.capstonekids.com

Look for all the books in this series!

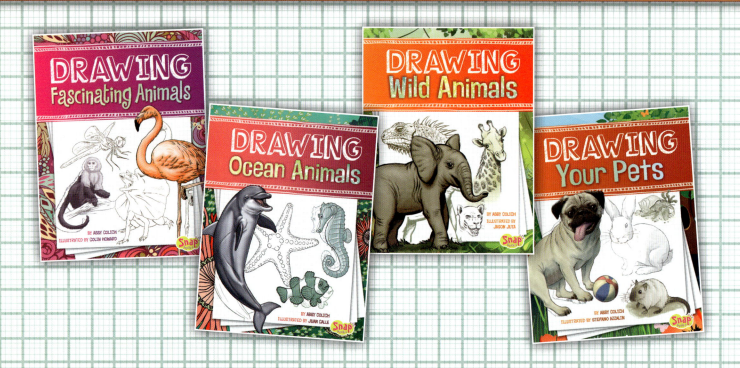